THE
AUDACITY
OF
SPEAKING
THE
TRUTH

A Compendium of Events Leading to the
2010 Mid-term Elections

Linda Rockford

ISBN: 1456550500
ISBN-13: 9781456550509

Dedicated to our U.S. military personnel whom
have sacrificed life and limb to preserve "life,
liberty, and the pursuit of happiness," as defined
by our Founding Fathers.

INTRODUCTION

August 15, 2010 – The day I begin to fulfill my pledge to write a book once I retired. I made this pledge to myself and to my husband. I've now been retired three years. So why has it taken so long to begin? One reason: I wavered on what kind of book to write, that is, fiction, non-fiction, biographical. Well, thanks to a dream I had last night—a dream that seemed to go on for hours—the answer became clear. I believe in dreams; I believe dreams have a purpose, most of which are never clearly understood.

Glenn Beck, author of *The Real America*, wrote, "I had a dream. I actually believe that it was more of a personal prompting than just a dream." Thanks to Mr. Beck, I'm acknowledging that my dream was "a personal prompting" by God. In fact, I asked God to help me remember the details so I could transfer specifics to paper. I was too lazy to get out of bed and write down the details—unlike Glenn Beck, who arose at 3:00 a.m. to "paint a picture because his dream was so vivid and its message so clear."

So, thanks to you, Mr. Beck, and thanks to you, God, I'm now inspired to listen to my soul, to listen to the Holy Spirit because God communicates with us through the Holy Spirit. Again, to quote Glenn Beck, "If I can write a book, have a company publish it, and people like you actually want to buy it, then anyone can."

My motivation for writing this book is not to make money; in fact, it'll most likely cost me more than I'll recover. My motivation is to fulfill a promise I made to my husband and to myself. It only took Glenn Beck and the Holy Spirit to get me started.

TABLE OF CONTENTS

Chapter 1

WHO AM I?

I was born on January 24, 1947, in Kansas City, MO, to a twenty-year-old woman who fell in love with a World War II hero, my father. Did I mention my father was a World War II hero? He was also a drunk who would leave my mother, two brothers, and me for days at a time without means to purchase groceries and other necessities. My first four years of life largely consisted of living with my maternal aunt, who was also married to a World War II veteran.

Because of my father's alcoholism, I knew very little of him. The few memories I do have consist of him screaming at me—like the time he tried to teach me how to spell my middle name, Anne. I insisted on spelling it "And." After he repeatedly yelled at me to convey how to spell "Anne," eventually it sunk in. Sadly, that is the only lesson I learned from him.

FAST FORWARD

My mother finally garnered the courage to divorce this excuse for a husband and save her three young children from what would surely have been a hellish life. She was also blessed to have friends who introduced her to another World War II veteran, whom she would eventually wed on December 4, 1954 in Southern California—a definite perk for my brothers and me. They later gave birth to a son the following September.

Their marriage lasted until Mom's death from Alzheimer's disease on Christmas Eve, 2003. This Marine veteran raised four kids and was a loving husband throughout their forty-nine-year married life.

I've always called him "Dad." He turned eighty-seven years old in February 2011.

SO WHAT?

You're probably yawning by now, thinking, "Why should I care about Linda's early years. Who is she to me?" You're absolutely right; I am nobody—but I'm going to finish writing this book anyway. The compulsion to write my story comes from a fire burning deep inside me. The fire is based on my deep love and respect for the United States of America. I've tried to recall when the passion I felt for my country began to well up within me, and I believe it was during the early 1970s when I read *Atlas Shrugged* by Ayn Rand. The message was clearly outlined by Ms. Rand that people who had a strong work ethic had the "duty" to "give" to people who felt "entitled" (I paraphrase, of course); that those who are willing to work hard had the moral obligation to "share their wealth" with the lazy ne'er-do-wells.

SOUND FAMILIAR?

Ayn Rand was born in Russia in February 1905, and *Atlas Shrugged* was published in 1957. Ms. Rand certainly had the credentials to write about Communist philosophy. It's noteworthy to mention that the progressive movement began over one hundred years ago. The goal was to destroy our churches, history, and Constitution. Today's administration—with the aid of the media—is advancing these goals. "Free enterprise" and "Capitalism" are dirty words, and our kids are being indoctrinated to believe this on all educational levels!

Today, the U.S.A. is governed by this same philosophy. Scary? You bet it is! It's not an original idea if you know the objectives of Woodrow Wilson, FDR, and LBJ. But, thank God, we had Ronald Reagan, who reminded us that because of our Founders' unbending belief in God Almighty, they crafted the most brilliantly written documents in all of U.S. history—they're known as the Declaration of Independence and the U.S. Constitution. Since President Reagan's two-terms, our government has tripled in size and our debt has skyrocketed to the point our grandchildren will be shouldered with paying it down. But I digress. The core of my fear—and the fear of millions of Americans—is that our country will disappear before its three hundredth anniversary. By the way, it took nearly eight hundred years for Rome to fall—but again, I digress. In less than 250 years, the U.S.A. became the most powerful country in the world—and the most democratic! How did we attain this status? Through our Judeo-Christian belief that "all men are created equal" and our willingness to work hard to achieve the American dream. The American dream is again under attack from the leftists, who want government to control how we live, work, and die.

During a recent panel discussion, Dennis Prager eloquently pointed out that "the single greatest threat to the future of our country is our failure to articulate to the younger generation what America actually stands for." Our educational system is at fault; our mothers and fathers are at fault. The younger generation is becoming like Europeans who are obsessed with entitlements—the length of their vacations, shorter work weeks, and early retirement.

WHERE ARE WE NOW?

When we approached retirement, my husband subtly planted the seed of relocating from Washington State to Mexico to live out our golden years. Initially, I resisted this idea of leaving my beloved country, but a couple of things happened to change my thinking. First, because of the greed and avarice of our company CEO, Joe Nacchio, my husband and I collectively lost over one million dollars in our 401K. The second motivating factor to leave the U.S. was Hillary Clinton. I told my husband, "I would leave the country if she won the presidential election." My husband secretly hoped she'd succeed, not because he admired her, but because he badly wanted to live on the beach—and Mexico was affordable. I couldn't know then that Hillary would lose the nomination to a person whose Socialist philosophy is more to the left of Hillary's—more about him later.

FROM BAD TO WORSE

We now know that Hillary lost the "big prize," but she's still very much alive and running the State Department. Barack Hussein Obama (BHO) did win the big prize; however, judging by his radical, autocratic, activist behavior, you'd think he was crowned King, a title George Washington was actually offered, but he rebuffed the notion. BHO has ignored our Constitution, has apologized for the U.S.A. to world leaders, has "bought" votes to pass universal healthcare, and has been unapologetic in carrying out his Socialist agenda. His transition from being an Illinois senator to president of the United States was meteoric, and historic, historic because of his ethnicity. In two short years, with the support of two Democratic controlled houses, BHO has managed to "fundamentally transform" our nation. And he's done so by ignoring our constitutional laws and the voice of America. I'll go on record to say that he would be impeached if we had a fair and unbiased government body.

Chapter 2

TEA TIME IN AMERICA

At my age, there a few "firsts" in life, but the Tea Party movement is certainly a first in my sixty-three years on this earth. The Tea Party movement is a fiscally conservative socio-political movement that began in early 2009. Barely three months into the current administration, this grassroots movement—comprised of common folks like you and me— began gathering at town meetings to express their outrage over being virtually ignored by government leaders. Initially there were forty-eight Tea Party protests nationwide. As of today, there are over two thousand Tea Party organizations represented in virtually every state in the Union. These patriots came together to protest numerous federal laws like the Emergency Economic Stabilization Act of 2008, the American Recovery and Reinvestment Act of 2009, the Federal Reserve Transparency Act, and a two thousand plus-page healthcare reform bill that no one read.

I repeat…no one read this massive bill! As the speaker of the House declared, "We need to pass the bill in order to know what's in it."

HEALTHCARE REFORM BILL

What's in it? The following are only a few of actual words that make up what is popularly known as "ObamaCare":

- Page 50/section 152: The bill will provide insurance to all non-U.S. residents even if they are here illegally.
- Page 58 and 59: The government will have real- time access to an individual's bank account and will have the authority to make electronic fund transfers from those accounts.
- Page 65/section 164: The plan will be subsidized (by the government) for all union members, union re-tirees, and for community organizations such as the Association of Community Organizations for Reform Now (ACORN).
- Page 203/lines 14-15: The tax imposed under this sec-tion will not be treated as a tax.
- Page 241 and 253: Doctors will be paid regardless of specialty, and the government will set all doctors' fees.
- Page 272/section 1145: Cancer hospitals will ration care according to the patient's age.
- Page 317 and 321: The government will impose a pro-hibition on hospital expansion; however, communities may petition for an exception.
- Page 425/lines 4-12: The government mandates ad-vance-care planning consultations. Those on Social Security will be required to attend an "end- of-life plan-ning" seminar every five years.
- Page 429/lines 13-25: The government will specify which doctors can write an end-of-life order.

Simply based on the few notable inclusions shown above, there's no doubt in my mind that only a handful of Americans have actually read this massive bill. Otherwise, there would certainly have been loud and vociferous protests heard from citizens in all fifty states. The final straw is that it turns out "the president, staff and family; the vice president, staff and family; speaker of the House, Senate majority leader, and their staffs; and all the cabinet officers—as well as Congressional Committee staff—were written out of the new HealthCare Act." Not only is this infuriatingly outrageous, it's also unconstitutional! Fortunately, the 112th Congress is actively meeting to repeal this outrageous law that is supported by less than 30 percent of U.S. citizens. Yes, BHO will exercise his power of veto should it make its way to the Oval Office, but the fight to repeal will continue.

Government-run healthcare was passed by Congress despite the protests of over 60 percent of American citizens. We were told that our health insurance premiums would decrease and "everyone" would have healthcare insurance. Not true. Insurance premiums began to climb almost immediately. Recently, large corporations declared the possibility of having to drop all health benefits because of the prohibitive expense.

Medical professionals have declared they'll leave their industry if this unconstitutional bill is not repealed. Stay tuned.

AUTOCRATIC DECISIONS

Banks and car companies were being taken over by the government at the discretion of the president. Billions of dollars were meted out to hundreds of non-revenue producing entities, dozens of which were "pay-offs" to lawmakers in order to get their vote to pass these bills. This is NOT the America in which I was raised!

According to the census bureau, as of September 2, 2010, deficit spending has increased by 16 percent. As of today, $1.5 trillion has been spent by the current administration compared to $1.3 billion three years ago. If this rate of spending continues, you and I will go bankrupt. Cause for anger? You bet. Contrary to government leaders (you know who they are), the Tea Party participants are not "radical right wing protesters." They are common folks who have been ignored by their government to the point of taking action on their own to voice their opposition to the actions of their government—high taxes, out-of-control spending, expansion of government, and rising unemployment, which has jumped to 9.6 percent as of 10/07/2010 (much higher in certain states).

Chapter 3

WASHINGTON D.C. 8/28/10

By now, you may have heard of Glenn Beck's remarkable feat in organizing one of the most important events ever to be held at the Lincoln Memorial. This experience will remain with me for a lifetime. The rally, "Restoring Honor," was attended by hundreds of thousands of people who traveled from across the nation. I know; I was there. To quote some media reports, for example, *CBS News*, "There were 87,000 people"; *The Washington Times*, "Tens of thousands of anti-government activists," *The Washington Post*, "The rally drew an enormous crowd," and *USA Today*, "Tens of thousands of people." According to Glenn Beck's *reliable* sources, there were at least 500,000 people. It's been said that this event drew the sixth largest crowd of all time, tied only with the inauguration of Ronald Reagan. The people lined the reflecting pool, which spans nearly a mile. People stood at the feet of the Lincoln Memorial, waving Old Glory as the sun shone brightly throughout the three-hour event (the temperature climbed to 96 degrees).

I arrived in D.C. late August 27 from Puerto Vallarta. Upon arriving at the hotel, I asked for a 6:00 a.m. wake-up call the next day; I wanted to be sure to get a good seat for the rally. When I arrived at the Metro station, I saw hundreds of people who had the same idea. Between 9:00 and 10:00 a.m., traffic was clogged throughout the District of Columbia, and subway lines stretched the length of two football fields. Metro officials said they had "never seen anything like it."

During the weeks prior to August 28, Glenn told us to "expect miracles." Well, I can attest that at 9:59 a.m., a flock of geese flew in V-formation over the site of the rally—9:59 a.m., one minute before the official start of the rally! Glenn said it was "divine providence." I agree.

Another notable fact is that these people came not to protest, but to listen to the speakers, whose messages trumpeted the theme of **faith**, **hope**, and **charity**. Appearing together on stage, arms linked one to the other, were 240 clergy of all faiths—rabbis, imams, priests, and pastors. They were referred to as the "black robe regiment." Also on stage was Alveda King, niece of Martin Luther King, Sarah Palin, former governor of Alaska, and several military heroes.

The event was non-political. For months, Glenn invited us to "come with an open heart and leave your signs at home… bring your children." The central theme was about God and prayer, to restore honor to America through faith, hope, and charity. Glenn spoke about the "forty days and forty nights challenge." He stressed that "everyone has a purpose," and to "believe in the reliance of divine providence." He said, "We need to turn back to God." I've often pondered the whys and wherefores of what led to the banning of prayer in public schools, the banning of public displays of Christmas nativity scenes, and so on. I came to the conclusion that if we Americans turn our backs on God, why should he not turn His back on us?

There was another rally taking place on August 28, led by Reverend Al Sharpton. They referred to their rally as "One Nation" and was billed as a "major event" and attended by representatives from virtually every leftist organization operating in America. Groups like the People's Organization for Progress, Progressive Democrats of America, Planned Parenthood, and People for the American Way were there. Many union members were **PAID** to attend. Although the rally turnout was lower than expected, what shocked me most was the fact that members of the "Communist Party USA" openly carried signs boldly announcing their propaganda.

Even more shocking was the way in which the Communists were embraced and welcomed by the "Progressives" (a nice name for liberal extremists) while many in the so-called mainstream media conveniently chose not to show their viewers footage of the Communist presence.

SOCIALIZATION OF AMERICA IS WELL UNDER WAY...
The Obama theme scheme of "change," as embraced by his radical Socialist cohorts and rammed down the collective throats of grassroots Americans, is designed to do one thing... To reshape America into a Socialist nation.

Chapter 4

BROKEN PROMISES

It seems that throughout history, mayhem and chaos have resulted from dishonest human beings projecting lies and false promises to the masses. In the two years that BHO has been commander-in-chief, he has broken many promises. Allow me to elaborate:

1) He promised to be the most transparent president in history and "make himself available to the press," yet at one point, he went over three hundred days without a press conference.

2) He promised that the public would have five days to look online to see the details of a bill before he signed it so we the people "would know what your government is doing." Yet, as early as April 2009, he had broken this five-day posting pledge at least ten times out of the eleven bills he actually signed.

3) He promised he would televise the healthcare debates on *C-SPAN* so Americans could see what choices were available, yet in the final weeks, he wouldn't even allow Republican leaders to participate—much less open the process to the TV cameras.

4) He promised bipartisanship, yet he consistently blocked the Republicans from the political process.

5) He promised to close the prison in Guantanamo Bay, saying the detention center "helped al Qaeda recruit

terrorists to its cause"—a contention never proved. Yet, in his third year term, the detention center is still operating. Speaking for myself, this is a broken promise that does not disappoint me. Bad men who want to kill Americans are there and, incidentally, live in better surroundings than they had in their homeland. It's been reported that of those detainees who were released, at least 40 percent returned to their terrorist camps with the goal to continue to kill Americans.

A promise BHO *has* lived up to is his vow to "fundamentally transform the United States of America." Has he succeeded in fulfilling his promise? If 9.8 percent unemployment, a projected $14 trillion dollar debt, record-breaking deficit spending, and blatant disregard for the U.S. Constitution fit your ideal for success, the answer is yes. BHO has skirted the Constitution on numerous occasions. He isn't concerned about "procedural" or "traditional" rules; he simply issues executive orders to achieve his agenda. He has appointed over thirty czars without congressional confirmation. By the way, the majority of these czars are self-proclaimed Communists, Marxists, and Socialists. Some have even praised Mao Tse Tung, a dictator responsible for the mass murder of millions of his own citizens who opposed him.

My parents raised me to believe that I would be judged by the company I kept. Take a look at the company BHO kept—before and now. How many of us have friends who bombed a federal building and lamented that he "couldn't bomb more"? How many of us attended a church for twenty years that was led by a fiery pastor who spouted hatred of the U.S.? I suspect few of us, but BHO is unapologetic for his life-long affiliations. Why would he be? He surrounds himself with these individuals because they mirror his thinking; they reflect his beliefs.

Recently, he appointed another individual, Elizabeth Warren, to head the new regulatory bureau, "Consumer Financial Protection." BHO described her as a "very close friend" who would set up this agency, which would then be turned over to a fulltime manager. Who is Elizabeth Warren? None of us knows, because she, like many advisors of BHO, has not been vetted.

If you're in favor of Obama's efforts to fundamentally transform America, you must be a Socialist who believes in the writings of Saul Alinsky and Cloward and Piven—or you simply hate America. (Are you listening George Soros?) You also don't care that our forty-fourth president surrounds himself with like-minded Socialists and Communists. I won't bother mentioning them by name because conservatives are well acquainted with their identities and goals to destroy the foundation upon which this great nation was built.

Chapter 5

IMMIGRATION

"Fathom the odd hypocrisy that Obama wants every citizen to prove they are insured, but people don't have to prove they are citizens!" – Ben Stein

Formerly, many developed countries conferred citizenship as freely as does the U.S. However, one by one, these countries came to recognize the folly of this policy. So, as of now, the only country that freely confers citizenship to babies born of illegal aliens is the United States of America. The developed countries that have terminated their birthright citizenship policy include Canada, Australia, New Zealand, Ireland, France, India, Portugal, and the United Kingdom. It's high time to include the United States on this list.

ARIZONA

In my lifetime, I don't know of an incident when the federal government filed suit against a state—until now. Eric Holder, the attorney general, under the direction of BHO, filed SB1070, the lawsuit against the sovereign state of Arizona to block the state from carrying out the immigration laws that had already been recognized as "federal law." Without precedent, our government sided with a foreign government against our own state! Didn't the president of the U.S. pledge to "protect citizens of America from foreign invaders"? Can it be true that

BHO has actually sided with a foreign country against one of its sovereign states? If this isn't an impeachable offense, what is? This is an attack on the citizens of Arizona and on every citizen of the U.S.

This administration has sided with a foreign country, Mexico, to sue Arizona for having the "gall" to enforce a federal law that the federal government refuses to enforce. As of this writing, eleven Latin American countries have joined Mexico and the U.S. government in fighting Arizona's efforts to enforce an immigration law that has already been recognized as federal law—a federal law that the current administration refuses to enforce.

For the last two years, the Arizona and Texas borders have experienced rampant murder and mayhem. Over thirty thousand drug-related murders have been committed and more than one-third of Arizona's prisoners are comprised of illegal aliens. If it wasn't for the courage of Arizona's governor, Jan Brewer, the state legislature may have caved in standing up to the federal government. Instead, Arizona is contesting this shameful lawsuit and is pursuing an aggressive campaign to enforce the federal law with the goal of ridding the state of crimes perpetrated upon their citizens by illegal aliens and drug cartels.

At least twenty state governments have followed the example of Arizona and are endorsing an Arizona-style crackdown on illegal immigrants. Will the White House file suit against these states? Stay tuned…

What happened to the inaugural oath to "protect and defend the citizens of the United States"? If this is Obama's idea of fulfilling that pledge, he's not fit to lead our country. That our federal government won't stand behind the laws they have enacted is reprehensible. This administration will go down in history as violating constitutional law when the law contradicted their agenda.

In August 2010, the Justice Department sued the state of Arizona on the basis of "racial profiling" in identifying people who were in the state without complying with immigration laws. They also filed another suit against Arizona saying, "The network of community colleges acted illegally in requiring non-citizens to provide green cards before they could be hired for jobs." The same law says, "If you hire an illegal alien, it's illegal." Illegal aliens have more rights than U.S. citizens. For example, if you're a U.S. citizen, you must show proper identification when:

- stopped by police;
- making purchases on a credit card;
- visiting a doctor's office or emergency room;
- filling out a credit card or loan application;
- applying for a driver's license;
- applying for any kind of insurance;
- applying for college;
- donating blood;
- making debit purchases, especially if out of state;   and
- collecting a boarding pass for an airline or train travel.

I'm sure I've overlooked more instances where Americans are required to prove their identity, but you get my drift.

Further evidence that insanity reigns in this administration! Wouldn't it be comforting if this administration would invest this much time and energy into fighting the wars in Iraq and Afghanistan? Or how about taking a strong stance against the Iranian maniac, Ahmadinejad, for vowing to "wipe Israel off the face of the map"? No—they'd rather attack our own state governments for doing what the federal government refuses to do.

Furthermore, as I write this, there's breaking news that Sheriff Joe Arpaio of Maricopa County, Arizona, has been sued by the feds for alleged discrimination against Hispanics (racial profiling). Sheriff Arpaio is a strong, conscientious individual who will carry out his duty according to the law, come hell or high water.

Why, then, would our federal government deign to sue him?

While we're on the subject of illegal aliens, Obama's aunt is living off taxpayers. She said it's her "right." She said, "I'm owed; you (America) are here to help people, the poor and other countries and me (women), and you have to give me my right." She said she wanted to stay in America but did nothing about it for the ten years while she collected disability checks and lived in public housing before being exposed. Our sitting president knew that a member of his family was an immigration law-breaker and welfare cheat, but did nothing about it, until recently, when a judge granted her asylum. This reminds me of his reaction to Acorn being exposed as an illegal institution that accepted government funding under false pretenses. When ABC's news commentator, George Stephanopoulos pointedly asked Obama about Acorn, he shrugged his shoulders, saying, "I don't follow that stuff." Really? I guess it slipped his mind that he was up to his eyebrows representing Acorn as a lawyer and community organizer before he became an Illinois senator.

DISCRIMINATION

Alaska – August 26, 2010 - A man was arrested at the Alaska State Fair in Palmer, Alaska. Why? He was toting a large sign that said, "Impeach Obama Now." Within a few yards of this incident were people selling t-shirts that had pro-Obama slogans emblazoned across the fabric—they were not intruded upon. Anyone who disagrees with the policies of Barack Obama is subject to being labeled as a racist, and could even be subject to arrest.

Chapter 6

SUMMER OF 2010

The "lame stream" media or "drive-by media"—to use phrases coined by Rush Limbaugh—have been complicit in aiding BHO to realize his goal of transforming America. Bernard Goldberg best described this wave of adoration in his best-selling book, *A Slobbering Love Affair, Starring Barack Obama.* Could this be one of the reasons BHO has taken seven vacations in less than two years? It's one way to avoid uncomfortable questions posed by real-life journalists. You may accuse me of being biased. If harboring a passion for liberty and freedom, as defined in the writings of our Founders, personally identifies me as being biased, it's a label I proudly proclaim.

THE ECONOMY

On Labor Day, 2010, BHO hit the campaign trail to promote yet another stimulus, this one totaling $50 billion. Of course, he insisted it's was not a "stimulus"; it's simply a bill to "create jobs." Really? When V.P. Joe Biden declared this to be "recovery summer," why would there be a need for yet another multi-billion dollar stimulus bill? Perhaps Mr. Biden was unaware that more than 283,000 jobs had been lost; the nation's unemployment had risen to 9.8 percent (Gallup poll said it's over 10 percent as of this writing), and that GDP growth was only 1.6 percent in the second quarter of 2010. Existing home sales were down 27 percent in July 2010.

Also a record 41.8 million Americans were recipients of food stamps—a shameful record to be certain.

According to Tim Kaine, DNC chairman, the GDP "is growing, albeit slowly." He went on to say, "We're slowly climbing out of the ditch on the ladder built by the Democrats." During the twentieth century, America was the most powerful, most open society in the world. Throughout the last half century, however, we worried about America's supremacy. The concept is well underway that America may be surpassed by another country like China; that America is in gradual decline. I prefer to embrace the words of Ronald Reagan, "That America's best days are before us."

How do we stop the madness of out-of-of control spending? Here's a revolutionary idea…for starters, let's fire all the czars, cease spending, extend the Bush tax-cuts, slash the enormous staff of Michelle Obama—who shouldn't have more than a staff of two in the first place—eliminate all earmarks on both sides of the aisle, outlaw the appropriation of taxes to fund personal travel of any elected official, and reduce the size of the government by at least 10 percent. As Congressman Ron Paul said, "Now is the time to fight back against the out of control Federal Reserve and continued Wall Street plundering of our tax dollars." It's time to audit the federal government!

The liberal left repeatedly blames George W. Bush for the current state of affairs, none more so than BHO. While many people have swallowed this nonsense, it's high time to pin the tail on the donkey (pun intended).

A small handful of genuine journalists have attempted to explain the role Pelosi's house played in creating the current financial debacle, but they're drowned out by the government-supported, lame-stream media pundits. Barney Frank and Chris Dodd, architects of the failed Fannie Mae and Freddie Mack agencies, have thus far escaped blame for their leadership roles. They, in truth, should be held legally accountable and incarcerated for their shameful actions. Thankfully, leaders like Michele Bachmann, Jim DeMint, Sarah Palin, John Boehner, Mitt Romney, and others, are unafraid to tell Americans the truth and lay out a specific plan to reclaim our nation from those who desire to destroy it. These individuals and others have voiced a common fact that "budgets do not come from the White House; they come from Congress," and the party that has controlled Congress since January 2007 is the Democratic Party. They controlled the budget process 2008, 2009, and 2010. Granted, in 2007, they had to contend with George W. Bush, which caused them to compromise on spending, but once GWB was gone, the spending floodgates were opened wide.

SOCIALISM

Current European Tax Rates:

United Kingdom
Income Tax: 50%
VAT: 17.5%; TOTAL: 67.5%

France
Income Tax: 40%
VAT: 19.6%; TOTAL: 59.6%

Greece
Income Tax: 40%
VAT: 25%; TOTAL: 65%

Spain
Income Tax: 45%
VAT: 16%; TOTAL: 61%

Portugal
Income Tax: 42%
VAT: 20%; TOTAL: 62%

Sweden
Income Tax: 55%
VAT: 25%; TOTAL: 80%

Norway
Income Tax: 54.3%
VAT: 25%; TOTAL: 79.3%

Netherlands
Income Tax: 52%
VAT: 19%; TOTAL: 71%

Denmark
Income Tax: 58%
VAT: 25%; TOTAL: 83%

Finland
Income Tax: 53%
VAT: 22%; TOTAL: 75%

If you've started to wonder what the real costs of Socialism are going to be once the full program in these United States hits your wallet, take a look at the table shown above.

As you digest these mind-boggling figures, keep in mind that in spite of these astronomical tax rates, these countries are still not financing their social welfare programs exclusively from tax revenues! They are deeply mired in public debt of gargantuan proportions. Greece has reached the point where its debt is so huge it is in imminent danger of defaulting. That is the reason the European economic community has intervened to bail them out. If you're following the financial news, you know Spain and Portugal are right behind Greece.

The United States is now heading down the same path. The VAT tax in the table is the national sales tax that Europeans pay. Stay tuned because that is exactly what you may expect to see the administration proposing after the fall elections. The initial percentage in the United States isn't going to be anywhere near the outrageous numbers you now see in Europe. Guess what? The current outrageous numbers in Europe didn't start out as outrageous either. They started out as miniscule—right around 1 percent or 2 percent, where they will start out in the United States. Magically, however, they ran up over the years to where they are now. If the liberal left get their way, expect the same circumstances here.

During my formative years, the notion that with hard work and perseverance, anybody could get ahead economically in the United States was true. With the possibility of tax rates spiraling upward between 60 percent and 80 percent, it's doubtful that the American dream can survive.

If our government taxes our citizens at a similar rate to Europe's, our lives will mirror life in Europe. We will be hard-pressed to buy a home. We will be hard-pressed to buy a car. We will be hard-pressed to send our children to college.

The battle cry of the Socialists will continue to trumpet the same message—equalize income, spread the wealth to the poor, and level the economic playing field.

They believe that accomplishing these goals will result in a better way of life. It's time to take a hard look at reality. Greece is a perfect example. Despite the Socialism system that has ruled this country for decades, with a 65 percent tax rate, they are drowning in public debt, would have defaulted without hundreds of billions in bailout money, and still 20 percent of their population lives in poverty.

What has all that Socialism money bought, besides ultimate power for the politicians running the show? Do you think these people are "free"? They're not. They are slaves to their economic "system."

THIS IS WHERE WE ARE HEADED UNLESS WE THROW OUT THE PRESENT LEFT WING CONGRESS AND OBAMA!

Chapter 7

PROGRESSIVISM

As I mentioned in a previous chapter, the Progressive movement began over one hundred years ago with the primary objective of destroying our churches, our history, and our Constitution. Under the current administration, we're well on our way to accomplishing these goals. Progressives are taking away our choices by convincing us it is for our own good. Daily manipulation is what is happening. Their answer to our current economic woes is to spend, spend, spend. If Progressives win, America loses—very simple. We're on our way to becoming a third world country if we don't wake up.

Eric Holdren, science czar, believes in "de-developing the U.S." He wants to regulate our way of life from the food we grow and consume to the sandcastles we build on our beaches. Incandescent light bulbs will be replaced by the new CFL light bulbs by 2012. Guess who's manufacturing these bulbs? The Chinese—not Americans. No job creation here.

ELITISTS PERCEPTION

Prior to the mid-term election, Congress became irrelevant. When BHO wanted to add a new regulation, he simply issued a presidential order or skirted the Constitution at will. By the way, our "first lady," Michelle Obama, supports all of these regulations. Yes, these Progressives are taking away our choices, all the while preaching that "it's for our own good."

History records the periods when innocent Japanese-Americans and German-Americans were rounded up and herded into enclosed camps "for their own good." This was done under the leadership of two Democrat presidents, FDR and Woodrow Wilson. These innocent citizens were abruptly uprooted from their homes without cause—simply because our government feared they may pose a threat to our security.

INDIVIDUAL LIBERTIES THREATENED

The American standard of life is changing. During the last eighteen months, new regulations have been passed to control our food choices, the soft drinks we consume, junk food limits, and even the amount of salt that can be used in the preparation of food in New York City restaurants. Private business transactions that result in $600 or more now require a form to be reported to the IRS.

In Georgia, a man grew vegetables and gave them away. He was fined $5000 because he "didn't have a license." California wants to begin regulating the size of television sets. Fast food outlets will soon be required to be located outside of school zones. Michigan home-based daycare providers are required to pay union dues when they're not even in the union. An Oregon senator recently proposed a tax credit for moms who breastfeed.

November 2010 – A Denair Middle School thirteen-year-old student was forced to remove an American flag from his bike because of complaints from some students. He told school authorities he "put the flag there as a show of support for the veterans in his family." Fortunately, this action spurred thousands of people nationwide—including military veterans—to protest the removal of the flag, and subsequently the thirteen-year-old was given approval to once again display Old Glory on his bike. Finally, there's good news for democracy.

THE MAN WHO BROKE THE BANK OF ENGLAND

Who's the driving force behind these ridiculous freedom-robbing regulations? One is the center for American Progress, a George Soros funded organization. Mr. Soros is not a patriot, nor is he a friend of freedom-loving Americans. He's an eighty-year-old billionaire who is funding organizations that are threatening the liberties for which Americans have sacrificed life and limb to preserve. One such organization is the Center for American Progress, which is against free enterprise and Capitalism.

Born of Jewish parents in Hungary in 1930, his name was George Schwartz. Because Jews suffered severe discrimination, at the age of six, his father changed their last name to Soros. At the age of fourteen, George pretended to be a non-Jew as he participated in the organized forced confiscation of property owned by Jews, many of whom were sent to death camps. Decades later, he intoned, "This was one of the happiest times of my life."

George Soros was behind the collapse of the British sterling, proudly proclaiming he made over $1 billion.

He brought down regimes and collapsed their currencies, and is now focusing his efforts to accomplish these same feats in the United States.

An avowed atheist, he's openly declared his resentment of Jews and provides financial support to organizations who are anti-Israel. He has donated $14 million to the American Constitution Society, which is devoted to changing the U.S. Constitution through the amendment process. He's tried to destroy *FOX News* by donating millions of dollars to competitive left-wing news outlets such as The *Huffington Post*. In his words, he's seeking the "orderly decline of the dollar." Now that the Federal Reserve has announced that $600 million will go toward monetizing our debt, Mr. Soros may get his wish.

He has been described as "an unscrupulous profiteer who sucks the blood from people." Well, this profiteer continues his goal to profit from the downfall of the U.S. To quote him, "The main obstacle to a stable and just world order is the United States." His plan to gain control and collapse our economy involves five steps:

1) Form a shadow government using humanitarianism as a "cover."
2) Control the airwaves.
3) Destabilize the state, weaken the government, and build anti-government public sentiment.

4)   Provoke an election crisis, voter fraud. (Remember Minnesota's senatorial recount until Al Franken was ultimately proclaimed the victor.)

5)   Stage massive demonstrations.

This worked for him in four other nations, so it should be no surprise that he's trying to apply the same strategy here. He's behind myriad subversive activities to bring down this country. And, by the way, he's been a guest of the White House at least four times since Obama took occupancy. This is yet one more example of the reason BHO should be judged by the company he keeps.

UNION BIAS

Union bosses are other culprits. They support the effort to create global redistribution of wealth. "Workers of the world unite" is their slogan. Union members are pawns of this government. If you're a paying member of a union, are you comfortable with your union leaders, and what they're doing on your behalf? Billions of dollars are going overseas instead of staying here to help the poor in the U.S. Household wealth is down $1.5 trillion; stocks are down almost $2 trillion. And now, Hillary Clinton wants $50 billion to ship cook stoves to Africa?

The recent Gulf oil spill resulted in BHO issuing a moratorium to cease all drilling at a cost of thousands of jobs. A judge overruled the moratorium, but the Department of Justice simply issued another moratorium. At a cost of up to $3.5 billion, the U.S. capped and permanently sealed 3500 deepwater wells of our own oil companies. So, while thousands of Americans are out of work, what does our leader do? He authorizes billions of dollars in loans to Mexico and Brazil to drill for oil in exactly the same areas that were shut down for drilling by Americans. This doesn't make sense unless you're an advocate of global re-distribution of wealth—the oil drilled by foreign countries can then be sold to America, thus furthering "environmental equality."

This action closed the door on our own companies. Smaller oil producers will incur a revenue loss estimated between $6 and $18 billion! This smacks of punishing U.S. workers while foreign countries are rewarded with work that should be accorded to U.S. industry.

U.S. redistribution of wealth is not only the goal of this president; global redistribution of wealth is also a primary objective of the elite agenda. U.S. citizens are experiencing the highest rate of unemployment in more than forty years. Housing and commercial real estate foreclosures are at an all-time high. In the meantime, our government has tripled in size and deficit spending continues to explode at an unsustainable rate. From the time of George Washington to Reagan's administration, the combined deficit was less than the deficit accrued during the first nineteen months of the current administration—and it's still growing, a statistic that is shameful and critical to the future of this great country. As of this writing, one in seven Americans is considered "poor." This is simply unacceptable. This is the largest single jump since tracking began in 1959.

Furthermore, the national debt is estimated to grow to $130 trillion in ten years. As of January 2011 the national debt rose to $14 trillion. Globally, the debt amounts to $60 trillion. Is anyone else outraged by these statistics? This administration seems to harbor contempt for Capitalism and for people who have worked hard to advance their position. Why do we allow anyone to tell us how much money we can earn? Why are we penalized if we exceed the magical yearly income of $250,000? What U.S. president in history has mandated a monetary ceiling of yearly income? Since when did we give the power to one person to dictate how much money we could earn? Why are we letting him get away with this?

Since BHO took office, we've increased the federal deficit by $1.3 trillion; 3.2 million jobs have been lost, and the GDP growth has only been 1.6 percent. According to current IRS data, capitol employees owed $9.3 million in back taxes by the end of 2009. Names were withheld; however, 638 capitol workers were identified by the IRS. I wonder if Secretary of the Treasury Geithner would care to comment.

GLOBAL WARMING SCAM

Whenever the liberals lose the argument to support their leftist agenda, they simply change the wording. "Global warming" is now referred to as "global climate disruption." It would be humorous if it weren't so outrageously accepted by people who have made millions of dollars perpetrating this hoax. Al Gore, the most ardent promoter of this inane cause, is the recipient of fame and fortune. He's increased his personal fortune fifty to one hundred times while residing in his multi-room mansion that uses ten times the electricity that you or I consume. *An Inconvenient Truth* was seen and believed by millions of empty-headed people who haven't a clue about the true causes of climate change. The travesty is that now the EPA has control over our choice of light bulbs, and coming soon, the appliances we will no longer be able to buy. We're being told what cars we should drive, what food we should consume, and more to come. Eric Holdren, science czar, is promoting environmental equality by forcing America to buy oil from other countries. Two hundred thousand "green" jobs have been created by this regime. The twenty-three hundred-page healthcare bill, written long before it was ever revealed, produced over four thousand pages of regulations, some of which are only now coming to light.

GROUND ZERO

The ninth anniversary of the most heinous and savage attack on U.S. soil was observed September 11, 2010. The majority of Americans regard this day as "a day to remember and never forget." In the midst of solemn observation, there is an all-out effort by Imam Feisal Abdul Rauf to build a mosque within a few yards of what is considered to be hallowed ground, hallowed by nearly three thousand innocent people who lost their lives the day nineteen radical Muslims hijacked American planes to fly into the World Trade Center's twin towers, the Pentagon, and a Pennsylvania field. This Imam claims the purpose of the mosque is to "build bridges to peace" but refuses to disclose the funding source for this proposed $100 million mosque. Within weeks of the attacks, he's also quoted as saying, "After 9/11, America is an accessory to what happened." In a recent talk show, he said, "To refuse the construction of Cordoba House could result in dire consequences." This sounds like a threat from this "man of peace."

AUSTRALIA'S JULIA GILLARD

The Prime Minister of Australia, Julia Gillard, has the right idea about Muslims, and she's not shy about voicing it. For the second time, Gillard angered some Australian Muslims by saying she supported spy agencies monitoring the nation's mosques. Reportedly, she said that Muslims who want to live under Sharia law should get out of Australia:

> Immigrants, not Australians, must adapt... take it or leave it. I am tired of this nation worrying about whether we are offending some individual or their culture. Since the terrorist attacks on Bali, we have experienced a surge in patriotism by the majority of Australians.

> This culture has been developed over two centuries of struggles, trials, and victories by millions of men and women who have sought freedom. We speak mainly English – not Spanish, Lebanese, Arabic, Chinese, Japanese, Russian, or any other language. Therefore, if you wish to become part of our society, learn the language!

> Most Australians believe in God. This is not some Christian, right wing, political push, but a fact, because Christian men and women, on

Christian principles, founded this nation, and this is clearly documented. It is certainly appropriate to display it on the walls of our schools. If God offends you, then I suggest you consider another part of the world as your new home, because God is part of our culture.

We will accept your beliefs and will not question why. All we ask is that you accept ours and live in harmony and peaceful enjoyment with us. This is OUR COUNTRY, OUR LAND, and OUR LIFESTYLE, and we will allow you every opportunity to enjoy all this. But once you are done complaining, whining, and griping about our flag, our pledge, our Christian beliefs, or our way of life, I highly encourage you to take advantage of one other great Australian freedom, THE RIGHT TO LEAVE! We didn't force you to come here; you asked to be here. So accept the country YOU accepted.

Ms. Gillard is a courageous leader, and Australians can be proud of her willingness to speak honestly and candidly. Where is **our** Julia Gillard? Which of our leaders have the guts to replicate her remarks? The current administration certainly can't or won't produce such a leader. Perhaps the 112th Congress will produce a leader who mirrors the fortitude of Ms. Gillard....

Chapter 8

CHANGE & HOPE

November 2, 2010 – Judgment day has arrived. Mid-term elections were held and voter turnout throughout the nation exceeded all previous mid-terms. Republicans reclaimed the House of Representatives by over sixty seats and came within six seats of controlling the Senate. Not since 1948 has there been a more dramatic swing in the House of Representatives. Many are saying that these results are a repudiation of Obama's radical Socialist agenda.

In addition to congressional and senatorial candidates bombarding media outlets for months, BHO spearheaded "selective" backyard and community groups, during which he actually declared, "It's time to take back America." This from the guy who's done everything possible to destroy the American dream.

So now, we have significant "change" that will pave the way to "hope" to remove by our electoral process the current occupant of the oval office in 2012.

Madam Speaker Pelosi is out; John Boehner is in! No more Nancy Pelosi, who, as Speaker of the House, had the lowest approval rating in history at 11 percent. Time to go, Nancy. Time to retire altogether. You're a complete and utter embarrassment to Americans. Unfortunately, Ms. Pelosi isn't ready to call it quits. Within three days of losing the House, she told *ABC* network's Diane Sawyer that "she had no regrets"; that she'd rate her four years as madam speaker as "a job well done." So, despite objections from members of her own party, she decided to run for House Minority Leader—and won.

Harry Reid held his Nevada seat and will continue as Senate Majority Leader, but his power will be diminished by the newly elected Republican senators. Reid's victory, like California's Barbara Boxer's, was largely due to the union members who want to continue to rake in the benefits denied to non-union members. After all, they paid him for this privilege.

Chapter 9

LAVISH TRIPS

Within three days of the trouncing of sitting Democrats who were soundly defeated by Republicans in the mid-term election, BHO left town for a ten-day tour of India and Asia. Not only was he criticized for ditching his party to deal with spinning the reason(s) for this monumental trouncing, major criticism emanated from both parties—as well as the American people—concerning the multi-million dollar expenses related to this ten-day odyssey. At a time when unemployment was edging 10 percent, deficit spending was in the billions of dollars, this president "of the people" virtually thumbed his nose at all of us as he and his elitist wife boarded the lavishly decorated Air Force One on November 6, 2010. With an escort of three aircraft and five helicopters, he and his huge entourage jetted off to Mumbai. Where's the outrage from Al Gore and his global warming minions concerning the carbon footprint created from the multiple aircraft utilized by this administration? No denouncements voiced from the hypocritical left. They're too busy collecting the millions of dollars they've raked in as a result of their crusade to "save the planet."

The *Daily Mail Reporter* printed, "Not since the days of the Pharaohs or the Roman Emperors has a head of state traveled in such pomp and expensive grandeur as [the] president of the United States of America." Some reports claimed that thirty-four ships, including two aircraft carriers, six hundred plus security personnel, and a gigantic G.M. Cadillac tank-like vehicle provided ultimate security to this leader and his vast entourage. While the White House declined to disclose actual costs to the taxpayers, some reports are capping this ten-day jaunt at nearly $200 million. If "timing is everything"—a philosophy I've long embraced—the timing for this unbelievably costly extravagance couldn't have been more poorly executed.

OBAMA DOWNGRADES AMERICA – AGAIN

During one of many speeches delivered by Obama to Asian leaders, he implicitly acknowledged that the U.S. will lose dominance in the global market. He made this comment almost in a triumphant manner! While he's endorsing the Federal Reserve's action in pumping trillions of dollars into our economy—an act that is arguably going to lead to the devaluation of the dollar—he's once again bad-mouthing the country he leads.

The *India Times* reported, "In the context of his efforts, Obama clearly sees that [the] econom[ies] of China and India will exceed that of the U.S." Obama favors globalization while he seems to seek the destruction of America's economic dominance by encouraging the outsourcing of American jobs to India, China, and other countries.

Indonesia has more Muslims than any other country in the world. During a speech to their leadership, Obama told them that he believed relations had improved between America and the Muslim world, but "we must strive to do better." This from our leader who professes to be a Christian—his actions portray otherwise.

CHRISTMAS HOLIDAYS FOR THE OBAMA'S

Another vacation cost American taxpayers upwards of **$1.5 million**.

- $63,000 to fly Michelle and daughters to Hawaii
- $134,000 for twenty-four White House staff to stay at home
- $1 million for return trip on Air Force One
- $38,000 for the "Winter White House" the president rented for his family on the beach
- $16,000 to rent beachfront homes for Secret
- Service and Navy Seals

Mr. Obama evoked anger and outrage after taking a twenty-man motorcade to visit a childhood friend during his lavish Christmas holiday in Hawaii. The ten-vehicle convoy drove the first family from his rental property in Kailua, across highways cleared of traffic and through a military community to reach his boyhood friend, Bobby Titcomb's beachfront house.

The extra cost of the excessive security levels demanded by the vacation-loving Mr. Obama have enraged his opponents, and even a few of his supporters.

Chapter 10

WHO IS HE?

Barack Hussein Obama has been president of the United States for over two-years, yet we still don't know *who he really* is. He has withheld details about his formative years in Indonesia, education specifics such as his GPA at Columbia and Harvard, and other information. What we DO know is the fact that he's appointed a host of tax cheats, lobbyists, and leftist radicals. We know about his past relationship with Acorn, the agency that is now defunct, but could be operating under a different name. We know who his "friends" are and were, including Bill Ayers, the activist member of the Weather Underground, who confessed that he has "no regrets" that he couldn't do more damage when he set bombs at the Pentagon in 1972. We know BHO patronized a church for twenty years led by a tyrannical, America-hating minister, Rev. Jeremiah Wright. We also know his voting record as Illinois Senator, which revealed his leftist views from fighting the war in Iraq to tax and spending. He was known to be the most radically liberal member in the Senate. Of course, his radical agenda as president is also well known, and this alone could qualify him as one of the most dishonest chief executives in the history of the United States.

One of the most frightening aspects of Obama's persona is his penchant for free-fall spending of the people's money. While he's unrelenting in his belief that $250,000 should be

the ceiling for individual income before imposing excessive taxation, he demonstrates no conscience in squander-
ing taxpayers' money for luxurious vacationing for him and
his wife. (Remember her multi-million dollar trek to Spain?)
In November 2010, he and Michelle were off to India for a
nine-day Asian odyssey at a cost of more millions of dollars of
taxpayer money (see Chapter 8). Is this couple for real? They
conduct themselves as self-proclaimed royalty rather than
paid servants of the people—at least he is; she just rides the
wave of entitlement.

Are they tone-deaf to the nation's economic woes? No, I
don't think so; they simply don't care. They are elitists, who are
above caring about the nation's woes; they truly feel they are
entitled to behave as they wish.

Barack Hussein Obama is described as the most arrogant,
narcissistic man who's ever occupied the Oval office with the
possible exception of his Democratic predecessor, Bill Clinton.
The Merriam-Webster Dictionary defines narcissism as: *ego-
centricity, egocentrism, egomania, egotism, egoism, navel-gazing, self-absorption, self-centeredness, self-concern, self-interest,
self-involvement, selfishness, selfness, self-preoccupation,
self-regard*

While there's no evidence of "navel-gazing," the other
adjectives are fairly descriptive of this elitist.

These personality traits were exposed myriad times during his first year as president. In his first State of the Union
address, he referred to himself 114 times; he said "I" ninety-six

times, and used "my" or "me" eighteen times. He's given 158 interviews, 411 speeches, conducted twenty-three town hall meetings, visited fifty-eight cities in thirty states, and made ten foreign trips to twenty-one nations. During his overseas travels, he made numerous speeches in which he made repeated apologies for the United States, thus leading to many pundits using the tag line – "the apology tour." He bowed to world leaders, yet virtually snubbed the Queen of England, giving her an iPod filled with audio versions of his speeches. He's shown aloofness to our allies while cozying up to dictators like Venezuela's Hugo Chavez. When he held a press conference the day after his Democratic Party received an historic shellacking by the Republicans in the recent mid-term elections, instead of showing humility, he took personal blame as "not doing a better job of communicating his message to the American people." He omitted mentioning that he visited Ohio at least eleven times during his presidency to promote ObamaCare and stump for Ohio candidates. During a subsequent CBS 60 Minutes interview, he audaciously declared that the Democrats' losses were due to "failed communication skills rather than a rejection of his policies."

Finally, what are his *true* religious beliefs? As an American who embraces freedom of religion, I don't care what Mr. Obama's religious beliefs consist of; however, I do care that he appears to be hypocritical about his beliefs. It's a matter of record that he embraces the Islamic world, that he bows to Muslim royalty, that he travels to Muslim countries without the company of his wife, that he's been photographed during the month of Ramadan without his wedding ring or watch (Muslims are forbidden from wearing jewelry during Ramadan). We know he hasn't gone to a Christian church since entering the White House because "he doesn't want to be the cause of any disruption"—chalk it up to another unconfirmed rumor about this mystery man.

Chapter 11

A NEW DAY IN AMERICA

January 5, 2011 marked the opening session of the 112th Congress – 242 Republicans and 193 Democrats. Republicans comprised the largest freshman class in ninety years to take control of the House of Representatives. John Boehner was installed as the fifty-third speaker of the House, replacing Nancy Pelosi, arguably the least popular speaker of the House in U.S. history.

The first order of business drafted by Republicans was the passage of a new set of rules that contained the requirement that "every bill have an explanation of constitutional authority backing that particular measure." In addition, the GOP posted their pledge to America to "roll back government spending to pre-stimulus, pre-bailout levels," saving us at least $100 billion in the first year alone.

The second order of business was to read the U.S. Constitution in its entirety on the floor of the House of Representatives. What a novel idea...to actually read aloud the words that govern our land! I wonder how many members are hearing the words of our Constitution for the first time? Hopefully, all members of Congress listened and learned, but I have my doubts.

The third order of business was to repeal ObamaCare—the massive healthcare bill "bought and paid for" by the Obama regime. Because Republicans control Congress, there's little doubt there are enough votes for repeal. The Senate, however, will be an up-hill challenge. Even if the Senate should vote to repeal this obscene bill, BHO will veto. My prediction is that the Supreme Court will be the final adjudicator. Based on the make-up of the nine justices, the outcome could be based on political bias as opposed to constitutional law.

Chapter 12

TUCSON TRAGEDY

On Saturday, January 8, 2011, an outdoor Tucson function was held at a shopping center for the purpose of meeting with constituents of Congresswoman Gabrielle Giffords. Shortly after the open-air meeting began, a lone gunman opened fire on individuals in attendance, including Ms. Giffords. Before the gunman could be overtaken and stopped by two individuals, six people were killed and fourteen injured. Among the dead was a nine-year-old, who, as the recently elected class president, was selected to attend the event. A federal judge was killed, as well as a staff member of Congresswoman Giffords and three other innocent victims.

The gunman was a 22 year old loner who met the congresswoman in 2007, and saved her form letter "thanking him for his visit" in his safe. A registered Independent, the gunman was described by medical professionals as a "classic paranoid schizophrenic." Fellow students described him as a "nut case"; they expressed fear that one day he'd appear in class with a gun.

Tucson's Sheriff Dupnic, a long-time advocate of liberal causes, publicly opined that the "rhetoric of violence and hate from the likes of Rush Limbaugh was to blame for the massacre." Before the profile of the shooter was revealed, before facts were revealed that he held disdain for Congresswoman

Giffords since 2007, and within minutes of this profane act, liberal political pundits and government representatives immediately launched a political attack on the Tea Party movement, including Sarah Palin, Glenn Beck, and FOX News, assigning blame for the mass shooting. Never mind that the Tea Party movement had not been created in 2007, that few people outside of the state of Alaska knew of Sarah Palin, and that Glenn Beck was a commentator on the liberal cable TV station *CNN*. But why should indisputable statistics stand in the way of the irresponsible American leftwing media spewing remarks that attacked right-wing conservatives as being the root cause of this rampage. Other than *FOX News*, no media outlet urged cautionary restraint in making accusatory remarks before ascertaining the facts. In fact, the opposite was the case. Senator Durbin, Congressman Clyburn, and many other government representatives rushed to judgment—all assessing the right-wing to be the cause of the violence on that eighth day of January in Tucson. President Obama joined his party by taking no action to quell the speculation that blame be focused on the right-wing commentators. As a matter of fact, he telephoned Sheriff Dupnic to "thank him for his efforts to respond to this incident." This was yet another example of Obama capitalizing on a national tragedy to benefit the goals of his Socialistic agenda.

I was one of many who thought his behavior to be hypocritical in view of his statements immediately following the Fort Hood massacre where Major Nidal Malik Hasan, a Muslim, killed thirteen people. Within minutes of that incident, Obama cautioned Americans to restrain from judgment until all the facts were known. No such words came from him concerning the Tucson massacre.

I applaud Bernie Goldberg's remarks in which he defined the actions of the left-wing media to be "a shallow, thoughtless agenda-driven dribble, masquerading as serious analysis and commentary." Right on, Bernie!

Chapter 13

GOD BLESS AMERICA

When I was seven years old, I was "selected" to lead the student body in my California grade school in the formal reciting the Pledge of Allegiance that included for the first time the phrase, "under God." Now, fifty-seven years later, that phrase is being challenged by atheists and the ACLU. Our currency, our Supreme Court, and countless other federal treasures embrace these words on our national structures and engraved images. The president of the United States, himself, has omitted the phrase "under God" on numerous occasions, which prompted a letter to Mr. Obama, dated December 6, 2010, which represented sixty-eight bipartisan members of the U.S. House of Representatives. This letter reminded the president that on several occasions, when citing words from the Declaration of Independence, he failed to recognize the source of "inalienable rights" as "God, our Creator." And, in citing our Pledge of Allegiance, he omitted the words, "under God" on more than one occasion. These sixty-eight leaders offered to meet with the president to discuss these omissions. As of January 2011, there has been no reported response by Mr. Obama.

Our nation has bowed to the will of the liberal left. We've abandoned prayer in public schools. We've succumbed to liberal pressure to outlaw Christmas trees, nativity scenes, and even—out of political correctness—refrain from saying,

"Merry Christmas." Once again, insanity prevails. It's insane to turn away from God—never more so than in these times. Our founders were firm believers in God Almighty, and it was God Almighty who made possible their plight. I'm not a preacher; I'm not a minister, but I do know for a fact that if we turn our back on God, He will turn his back on us...and, we've never needed God to be on our side more than we do today.

VETERANS DAY, 2010

Obama was halfway around the world, making speeches in Indonesia, South Korea, India, and Jakarta. In his remarks to the citizens of Indonesia, he told them, "Americans must stop mistrusting Islam." Other than laying a wreath in honor of veterans at an Army base in South Korea on Veterans Day eve, he's made no remarks about the sacrifices made by America's military men and women. He did, however, laud those who "have sacrificed on behalf of this great country," the country being Jakarta. His arrogant aloofness prevails at a time when his approval ratings continue to fall, and for good reason.

ISRAEL AND PALESTINE

Hillary Clinton announced that the U.S. transferred $150 million in new aid to the Palestinian Authority to help close its budget gap. "This new funding will help the Palestinian Authority pay down its debt, continue to deliver services and security to its people, and keep the progress going," she said. "It will support our work together to expand Palestinians' access to schools, clinics, and clean drinking water in both the West Bank and Gaza Strip." Overall support and investment to the Palestinians is nearly $600 million for the 2010 year.

This announcement was made one day before the scheduled November meeting with Israeli Prime Minister Benjamin Netanyahu in New York. They were meeting to discuss the impasse in the Israeli-Palestinian peace process amid tensions over Israel's resumption of settlement construction. Clinton said that the Israeli decision to build thirteen hundred new apartments in East Jerusalem was "counterproductive" to the peace talks. Mr. Netanyahu's office insisted that "Jerusalem is not a settlement; it is the capital of the state of Israel." Despite the pressure from Palestinian President Mahmoud Abbas and Secretary Clinton to halt construction, building of the apartments has resumed.

Throughout my life, Israel has been considered a special friend of the United States—until now. When Netanyahu visited the White House earlier this year, Obama treated him like an unwelcome guest. This treatment continues as we continue to pour millions of dollars into the coffers of the Palestinians. In the meantime, Israel is derided and insulted by Iran's Ahmadinejad, whose goal is to "wipe Israel off the face of the map." It's no secret that Iran has been building a bomb that will have the capability to achieve mass destruction, so it's only a matter of time before armed conflict erupts between these two countries. I wonder which side the U.S. will take?

THE UNITED KINGDOM

Also throughout my life, one of our most loyal allies has been England. From the days of Winston Churchill through the years of Maggie Thatcher and Tony Blair, the U.S. and Great Britain's leadership enjoyed special camaraderie. Indeed, since the 1953 coronation of Queen Elizabeth, no country was held in more esteem than the U.K. Sadly, this tradition has been compromised by the actions of President Obama. According to the *London Daily Telegraph*, "One of the most poorly kept secrets in Washington is President Obama's animosity toward Great Britain." One of Barack Hussein Obama's first acts as president was to return to Britain a bust of Winston Churchill that had graced the Oval Office since September 11, 2001. He followed this up by denying Prime Minister Gordon Brown—on his first state visit—the usual joint press conference with flags. Aides of Mr. Brown told British journalists, "The president was too tired to grant the leader of America's closest ally a proper welcome." Obama followed this up with cheesy gifts for Mr. Brown and the Queen, such as an iPod containing Obama's speeches. Columnist David Hughes characterized Obama's behavior as being "unforgivable churlishness." I wonder if the Obama's will be on the guest list for Prince Williams April 29 wedding.

For the first time in a very long time, the president of the United States is actually distrusted by its allies and not in the least feared by its adversaries. I'll go one further...Obama has lost the respect of the majority of Americans.

Chapter 14

FINAL THOUGHTS

During the process of researching material contained in this book, I've been in a perpetual state of anger. I'm angry that our country has fallen into the hands of people who want to rob Americans of "life, liberty, and the pursuit of happiness." I'm angry that our Constitution is at risk of being rewritten at the whim of social activists; and I'm furious that our president continues to belittle, degrade, and apologize for America.

I'm looking for answers; I want to know what the hell is wrong with all the people who run this country! We're broke; we can't help our seniors, our homeless, our veterans, our orphans. Yet, Obama has provided financial aid totaling billions of dollars to Haiti, Chili, Turkey, and Pakistan, the home of Osama Bin Laden.

First Lady Michelle Obama recently hired another staff member – I believe this makes 14 – to act as her personal shopper. Remember, you and I pay their salaries. It's time for the Obama's to cease behaving like royalty and stop the spending on their personal extravagances.

If you read this book, I hope it made you mad as hell, mad enough to take action against the elites who want to destroy our way of life. I am hopeful that the results of the mid-term elections will mark the turning point of getting back the nation in which I was raised. I am also hopeful that the results of the 2012 election will mark the denouncement of Socialism and that we'll return to free enterprise and the embracement of Capitalism. If this does not occur, God help us all—at least those of us who believe in God.

For too long we have been complacent about the workings of Congress. Many citizens have no idea that members of Congress can retire with the same pay after only one term, that they specifically exempted themselves from any of the laws they passed that affect you and me, such as Healthcare Reform. Regardless of your party affiliation, the proposed Twenty-eighth Amendment should be ratified NOW. The amendment contains a simple message:

"Congress shall make no law that applies to the citizens of the United States that does not apply equally to the Senators and/or Representatives, and Congress shall make no law that applies to the Senators and/or Representatives that does not apply equally to the citizens of the United States."

The Twenty-sixth Amendment, which granted the right to vote to eighteen-year-olds, took only three months and eight days to be ratified in 1971. Now, forty years later, I believe the Twenty-eighth Amendment could be ratified in record time.

I wrote this book to fulfill a dream and commitment I made to God, my husband, and myself. In so doing, I realized my purpose for being alive at this point in time. For anyone who reads my book, this is my wish for you: That you realize your purpose and strive to fulfill it. Remember, "one person can make a difference"—just ask anyone who's read the biography of George Washington and Abe Lincoln.

In summary, I ask you to consider the following:

If any other of our presidents had doubled the national debt in one year, which had taken more than two centuries to accumulate, would you have approved?

If any other of our presidents had then proposed to double the debt within ten years, would you have approved?

If any other of our presidents had criticized a state law that he admitted he had never read, would you deem him to be an ignorant hot-head?

If any other of our presidents had joined a foreign country and sued a sovereign state of the U.S. to force that state to continue to allow illegal immigration, would you question his patriotism?

If any other of our presidents had pronounced the Marine Corps as Marine "corpse", would you think him an idiot?

If any other of our presidents had put 87,000 U.S. workers out of work by arbitrarily placing a moratorium on off-shore oil drilling, would you have agreed?

If any other of our presidents had used a forged document as the basis of the moratorium that rendered unemployment for 87,000 American workers, would you support him?

If any other of our presidents had been the first president to require that a teleprompter be installed in order to get through a press conference, would you have laughed at this being more proof of how inept he is?

If any other of our presidents had spent hundreds of thousands of our tax dollars to take his wife to a play in NYC, would you have approved?

If any other of our presidents had reduced your retirement plan holdings of GM stock by 90% and given the unions a majority stake in GM, would you have approved?

If any other of our presidents had bowed to the King of Saudi Arabia, would you have approved?

If any other of our presidents had visited Austria and made reference to the nonexistent "Austrian language", would you have brushed it off as a minor slip of the tongue?

If any other of our presidents had filled his cabinet and circle of advisors with avowed Communists, Marxists and Socialists, would you have approved?

If any other of our presidents had stated there were "57 states in the U.S.", would you question his capabilities?

If any other of our presidents refused to disclose his birth certificate, would you look the other way?

If any other of our presidents would have flown all the way to Denmark to make a five minute speech as to how it would benefit his hometown if it were selected to host the Olympics, would you consider him to be an egotistical jerk?

If any other of our presidents had burned 9,000 gallons of jet fuel to plant a single tree on behalf of Earth Day, would you conclude that he's a hypocrite?

If any other of our presidents had been so Spanish illiterate as to refer to Cinco de Mayo as "Cinco de Cuatro" when addressing the Mexican ambassador – then continued to flub it, would you wince in embarrassment?

If any other of our presidents had treated our closest allies such as Israel with such disdain, while catering to dictators such as Chavez and Islamic leaders, would you be alarmed?

So you may ask, what is it about Obama that makes him seem so brilliant and impressive? Can't think of an answer? Well, don't worry; he's done all of this and more in just 24 months, so there's still time to come up with an answer. But also remember this – "All it takes for evil to triumph is for good men to do nothing".

ACKNOWLEDGMENTS

There are numerous heroes that should be mentioned, beginning with the military men and women who are enduring unimaginable strife on an hourly basis to keep the enemy away from our shores. The others who warrant honorable mention include Rush Limbaugh, Matt Drudge, Glenn Beck, Sean Hannity, Mark Levin, Michael Savage, and all the FOX News contributors who are "unafraid" to speak the truth. Last but far from least, kudos to my many friends who continue to share what's really going on in our great nation and how our freedoms are gradually disappearing—you know who you are.

FOOTNOTE

In the dream I described at the beginning of this very short book, part of the dream was me interviewing a fifteen-year-old girl (I don't know any fifteen-year-old girls or boys). In the dream I asked her pointed questions about her views of what has happened to our country. Her answers were not specific, but my "dream" interpretation was that she was optimistic about her future. Was God telling me to "go out and talk to young people?" I don't know; but if so, I'll need to do so via the Internet since fifteen-year-old U.S. citizens are scarce in Mexico. Maybe this could be the theme of my next book. We'll see.